Thought you might

like this as it is

American

Love
Barry & Chris

**Let Summer begin!**

**Just like you,** the staff at the Kraft Creative Kitchens realizes meals are more casual and spontaneous in the summer than at any other time of the year. Regular meals become more relaxed. Children take a break from playing to have a sweet treat. Friends gather together after a softball game for an impromptu cookout. That's why the Kraft Creative Kitchens has compiled this enticing collection of warm-weather recipes.

To help you with summer meals, **NO OVEN SUMMER™** *Sensations* is filled with delectable recipes that are simple to fix and, even better, don't require oven cooking. What's more, sprinkled throughout this book, you'll find personal tips and hints from Kraft home economists for easy summer cooking.

For more than 70 years, the Kraft Creative Kitchens has delivered good food and good food ideas. And because every Kraft recipe is kitchen-tested by dedicated Kraft home economists, you can be assured of delicious and successful results each and every time.

This summer, enjoy the best in family favorites from Kraft.

*Pictured on front cover: Ranch Taco Chicken Salad (recipe, page 52)*

*Meat and Potatoes Salad (recipe, page 85)*

# NO OVEN SUMMER™
# Sensations

memorial *Backyard*

BBQ Bacon Cheeseburgers (recipe, page 7) and
Great American Potato Salad (recipe, page 8)

# day BBQ

The perfect way to celebrate Memorial Day is with a barbecue! Our Kraft Creative Kitchens has put together this NO OVEN SUMMER™ menu to keep your time in the kitchen to a minimum, plus it's guaranteed to please your family and friends.

## BACKYARD BBQ Menu

VELVEETA® Salsa Dip

BBQ Bacon Cheeseburgers

Easy Wrap Sandwich

BBQ Ranch Chicken Salad

Great American Potato Salad

JELL-O® Strawberry Gelatin Pops

JELL-O® Creamy Chocolate Pudding Pops

JELL-O® Frozen No Bake Peanut Butter Cups

PHILLY® Cheesecake Creme Parfaits

(see index for recipe page numbers)

# VELVEETA® SALSA DIP

*As an alternative to using the microwave, prepare this cheesy dip on top of the stove. Just stir together the ingredients in a medium saucepan over medium heat for about 5 minutes.*

Prep time: 5 minutes   Microwave time: 5 minutes

1   pound (16 ounces) VELVEETA Pasteurized Process Cheese Spread, cut up
1   cup TACO BELL HOME ORIGINALS Thick 'N Chunky Salsa

**MICROWAVE** process cheese spread and salsa in 1½-quart microwavable bowl on HIGH 5 minutes or until process cheese spread is melted, stirring after 3 minutes. Garnish with pepper knots. Serve hot with assorted tortilla chips or cut-up vegetables. Makes 3 cups.

VELVEETA® Cheesy Chili Dip: Substitute 1 can (15 ounces) chili for salsa. Serve hot with tortilla chips, French bread chunks and corn bread sticks. Makes 3¾ cups.

*TACO BELL and HOME ORIGINALS are trademarks owned and licensed by Taco Bell Corp.*

*VELVEETA® Salsa Dip*

*Denise Henderson
Kraft Creative Kitchens—
Glenview, Illinois*

## Quick tip

Whenever I serve grilled burgers and hot dogs, my guests always enjoy piling on their own toppings. To make this more fun, I set up a toppings buffet bar with ketchup and mustard, of course, and a variety of salsas, chopped veggies and cheese.

## BBQ BACON CHEESEBURGERS

*When removing these juicy patties from the grill, be sure to transfer them to a clean plate. To ensure food safety, never place cooked food on a plate that had raw food on it (photo, pages 4–5).*

Prep time: 15 minutes   Grilling time: 12 minutes

1   pound ground beef
2   tablespoons KRAFT Original
      Barbecue Sauce
8   KRAFT Deluxe Pasteurized Process
      American Cheese Slices
4   Kaiser *or* hamburger rolls, split,
      toasted
      Lettuce
8   slices OSCAR MAYER Bacon,
      crisply cooked

**MIX** meat and barbecue sauce. Shape into 4 patties.

**PLACE** patties on grill over hot coals. Grill 8 to 12 minutes or to desired doneness, turning and brushing occasionally with additional barbecue sauce.

**TOP** each patty with 2 process cheese slices. Continue grilling until process cheese is melted. Fill rolls with lettuce, cheeseburgers and bacon. Makes 4 sandwiches.

Backyard BBQ

## EASY WRAP SANDWICH

*For an easy appetizer, instead of folding up the sides of the tortilla, roll it up securely. Wrap in plastic wrap and refrigerate until ready to serve. Then, unwrap, insert toothpicks 1 inch apart and slice between the toothpicks (photo, at right and pages 16–17).*

KRAFT Mayo Real Mayonnaise *or*
  MIRACLE WHIP Salad Dressing
Flour tortilla
Lettuce
CLAUSSEN Kosher Dill
  Sandwich Slices
KRAFT Singles Process
  Cheese Food
OSCAR MAYER Smoked
  Cooked Ham

**SPREAD** mayo on tortilla.

**TOP** with lettuce, pickles, process cheese food and ham. Fold up sides of tortilla to center, slightly overlapping. Secure with garnished toothpick, if desired.

Easy Wrap Sandwich with Turkey: Substitute LOUIS RICH Oven Roasted Turkey Breast for ham and TACO BELL HOME ORIGINALS Thick 'N Chunky Salsa for pickles.

*TACO BELL and HOME ORIGINALS are trademarks owned and licensed by Taco Bell Corp.*

## GREAT AMERICAN POTATO SALAD

*Combine just six simple ingredients and you've got a fabulous homemade potato salad that no deli can beat (photo, pages 4–5)!*

Prep time: 20 minutes plus refrigerating

¾ cup MIRACLE WHIP *or*
  MIRACLE WHIP LIGHT Dressing
1 teaspoon KRAFT Pure Prepared
  Mustard
¼ teaspoon celery seed
4 cups cubed cooked potatoes
  (about 1½ pounds)
½ cup *each* CLAUSSEN Sweet Pickle
  Relish and sliced celery
Salt and pepper

**MIX** dressing, mustard and celery seed in large bowl.

**ADD** potatoes, relish and celery; mix lightly. Season to taste with salt and pepper. Refrigerate. Makes 6 servings.

*Easy Wrap Sandwich*

## BBQ RANCH CHICKEN SALAD

*For best results, serve this tangy salad immediately after assembling it.*

Prep time: 15 minutes   Cooking time: 8 minutes

- 1 pound boneless skinless chicken breasts, cut into strips
- ½ cup KRAFT Original Barbecue Sauce
- 1 package (10 ounces) salad greens
- 1 large tomato, cut into wedges
- ½ cup sliced red onion
- ½ cup KRAFT Ranch Dressing
- ¼ cup crumbled blue cheese

COOK and stir chicken in barbecue sauce in large skillet on medium-high heat 8 minutes or until chicken is cooked through. Add additional barbecue sauce, if desired.

TOSS greens, tomato and onion in large bowl. Top with chicken. Pour dressing over greens mixture. Sprinkle with cheese. Makes 6 servings.

Grilled Ranch Chicken Salad:
Place boneless skinless chicken breasts on greased grill over hot coals. Grill 14 to 18 minutes or until cooked through, turning and brushing occasionally with barbecue sauce. Slice chicken; serve over greens mixture.

*BBQ Ranch Chicken Salad*

# Day

## JELL-O® Strawberry Gelatin Pops

*These refreshing snacks are as easy to make as they are fun to eat. Try layering two flavors of JELL-O; freeze the first flavor before adding the second (photo, page 13).*

☀ Prep time: 10 minutes   Freezing time: 5 hours

- 1 cup boiling water
- 1 package (4-serving size) JELL-O Strawberry Flavor Gelatin Dessert
- ⅓ cup sugar
- 1⅓ cups cold water

**STIR** boiling water into gelatin and sugar in medium bowl at least 2 minutes until completely dissolved. Stir in cold water.

**POUR** into 5-ounce paper cups. Insert pop stick into each cup for handle.

**FREEZE** 5 hours or overnight until firm. To remove pops from cups, place bottoms of cups under warm running water for 15 seconds. Press firmly on bottoms of cups to release pops. (Do not twist or pull pop sticks.) Store leftover pops in freezer. Makes 6.

## JELL-O® CREAMY CHOCOLATE PUDDING POPS

*Tailor these frozen pudding pops to suit your fancy—use any flavor of JELL-O Instant Pudding & Pie Filling.*

Prep time: 10 minutes   Freezing time: 5 hours

- 2 cups cold milk
- 1 package (4-serving size) JELL-O Chocolate Flavor Instant Pudding & Pie Filling
- 1 cup thawed COOL WHIP Whipped Topping

POUR cold milk into medium bowl. Add pudding mix. Beat with wire whisk 1 minute. Stir in whipped topping.

SPOON into 5-ounce paper cups. Insert pop stick into each cup for handle.

FREEZE 5 hours or overnight until firm. To remove pops from cups, place bottoms of cups under warm running water for 15 seconds. Press firmly on bottoms of cups to release pops. (Do not twist or pull pop sticks.) Store leftover pops in freezer. Makes 6.

*JELL-O® Strawberry Gelatin Pops (recipe, page 11)
and JELL-O® Creamy Chocolate Pudding Pops*

# JELL-O® FROZEN NO BAKE PEANUT BUTTER CUPS

*The irresistible combination of peanut butter and chocolate make this frozen snack popular with kids and adults alike.*

Prep time: 15 minutes   Freezing time: 2 hours

- 1 package (16.1 ounces) JELL-O No Bake Peanut Butter Cup Dessert
- 1/3 cup melted margarine
- 1 1/3 cups cold milk

**PREPARE** Crust Mix as directed on package in medium bowl. Press onto bottoms of 12 to 15 foil-cup-lined muffin cups (about 1 heaping tablespoon per muffin cup).

**PREPARE** Filling Mix as directed on package in deep, medium bowl. Divide filling among muffin cups. Place Topping Pouch in hot water 30 seconds. Knead pouch 30 seconds. Squeeze topping equally over cups.

**FREEZE** 2 hours or until firm. Store, covered, in freezer up to 2 weeks. Makes 12 to 15 cups.

JELL-O® Frozen No Bake Cookies & Creme Cups: Prepare JELL-O No Bake Double Layer Cookies & Creme Dessert as directed on package, pressing prepared crust mixture onto bottoms of 12 foil-cup-lined muffin cups. Divide prepared filling mixture among cups. Top with reserved cookies. Freeze and store as directed above. Makes 12.

## PHILLY® CHEESECAKE CREME PARFAITS

*Now you can enjoy a creamy dessert in just a few cool minutes! Peaches, kiwi and raspberries also taste great in these parfaits.*

☀ Prep time: 5 minutes plus refrigerating

- 1 package (8 ounces) PHILADELPHIA Cream Cheese, softened
- 1 jar (7 ounces) marshmallow creme
- 1 cup *each* sliced strawberries and blueberries

`MIX` cream cheese and marshmallow creme until well blended. Refrigerate.

`LAYER` fruit with cream cheese mixture in dessert dishes or wine glasses. Garnish with fresh mint leaves and orange slice. Makes 4 servings.

PHILLY® Cheesecake Creme Dip: Mix cream cheese and marshmallow creme as directed. Serve as a dip with fresh fruit *or* pound cake cubes. Makes 1⅔ cups.

# Memorial Day

**Celebrate the nation's birthday with an old-fashioned potluck picnic. Whether your festivities are at a park, in a backyard or on a street at a block party, each of these tasty dishes is easy to make and to tote.**

4th of

## POTLUCK PICNIC
### Menu
Caesar Dip

Easy Taco Salad

Easy Wrap Sandwich

Simple Summer Marinade

Crunchy Bacon Coleslaw

PHILLY® No-Bake Cheesecake

Quick Vanilla Rice Pudding

JELL-O® Frozen Pudding and
Gelatin Snacks

(see index for recipe page numbers)

# July Potluck Picnic

Easy Wrap Sandwich (recipe, page 8) and
Crunchy Bacon Coleslaw (recipe, page 20)

## CAESAR DIP

*For a change of pace, serve this flavorful dip with colorful vegetables,
such as chunks or strips of red, yellow or orange bell peppers.*

☀ Prep time: 10 minutes

1   package (8 ounces)
    PHILADELPHIA Cream Cheese,
    softened
1   cup (4 ounces) KRAFT 100%
    Grated Parmesan Cheese
½   cup KRAFT Classic Caesar
    Dressing
1   cup chopped romaine lettuce
½   cup croutons

**BEAT** cream cheese, Parmesan
cheese and dressing with electric
mixer on medium speed until
well blended.

**SPREAD** on bottom of 9-inch
pie plate. Top with lettuce and
croutons. Sprinkle with additional
Parmesan cheese, if desired.
Garnish with lemon wedges.
Serve with crackers. Makes 2 cups.

## EASY TACO SALAD

*As a time saver, prepare the ground beef and salsa mixture the night before, refrigerate, reheat in the microwave oven and layer on the salad.*

☀ Prep time: 10 minutes   Cooking time: 10 minutes

1   pound ground beef
½   cup TACO BELL HOME ORIGINALS
    Thick 'N Chunky Salsa
4   cups shredded lettuce
    Tortilla chips
1   cup KRAFT Four Cheese Mexican
    Style Shredded Cheese

**BROWN** meat; drain. Stir in salsa.

**LAYER** lettuce, chips, meat mixture and cheese on large platter or individual serving plates. Top with chopped tomato and sour cream, if desired. Garnish with green onion curls. Makes 4 servings.

*TACO BELL and HOME ORIGINALS are trademarks owned and licensed by Taco Bell Corp.*

4th of July

## CRUNCHY BACON COLESLAW

*When purchasing the cabbage, keep in mind that a 1-pound head will yield about 4 cups of shredded cabbage (photo, pages 16–17).*

☀ Prep time: 15 minutes plus refrigerating

- ¾ cup MIRACLE WHIP *or* MIRACLE WHIP LIGHT Dressing
- 1 tablespoon sugar
- 1½ teaspoons cider vinegar
- 4 cups shredded green cabbage
- 1 cup shredded red cabbage
- ½ cup chopped peanuts
- 4 slices OSCAR MAYER Bacon, crisply cooked, crumbled

`MIX` dressing, sugar and vinegar in large bowl.

`ADD` remaining ingredients; mix lightly. Refrigerate. Serve in lettuce-lined bowl. Makes 10 servings or about 4 cups.

**Quick Crunchy Bacon Coleslaw:**
Substitute 1 package (8 ounces) coleslaw blend for shredded green and red cabbage. Substitute 1 can (3 ounces) OSCAR MAYER Real Bacon Bits for bacon slices.

**Crunchy Carrot Bacon Coleslaw:**
Add ¼ cup shredded carrot.

## SIMPLE SUMMER MARINADE

*Besides giving a flavor boost, this zesty marinade also makes chicken extra juicy (photo, back cover).*

☀ Prep time: 10 minutes plus marinating
Grilling time: 40 minutes

- 1 envelope GOOD SEASONS Salad Dressing Mix, any variety
- 1 broiler-fryer chicken, cut up (3 to 3½ pounds)

`PREPARE` salad dressing mix as directed on envelope.

`POUR` over chicken; cover. Refrigerate several hours to overnight to marinate. Drain; discard dressing.

`PLACE` chicken on greased grill over medium-hot coals. Grill, covered, 35 to 40 minutes or until chicken is cooked through, turning occasionally. Makes 4 servings.

NOTE: If using a combination of meat and vegetables, marinate in separate containers.

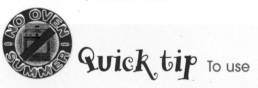

**Quick tip** To use Simple Summer Marinade on other meats and vegetables, use the following amounts and timings.

| Meat or Vegetable | Amount to Marinate | Time to Marinate (in refrigerator) |
| --- | --- | --- |
| Chicken (boneless) | 1¼ pounds | 1 hour to overnight |
| Beef | 1 pound | 4 hours to overnight |
| Fish | 1 pound | 30 minutes to 1 hour |
| Vegetables | 1½ pounds | 30 minutes to 1 hour |

*Chicken with Simple Summer Marinade*

# PHILLY® No-Bake Cheesecake

*To quickly soften the cream cheese, simply place the unwrapped cream cheese in a microwavable bowl and microwave on HIGH for 15 seconds.*

☀ Prep time: 10 minutes plus refrigerating

1 package (8 ounces) PHILADELPHIA Cream Cheese, softened
⅓ cup sugar
1 tub (8 ounces) COOL WHIP Whipped Topping, thawed
1 prepared graham cracker crumb crust (6 ounces *or* 9 inches)*

**MIX** cream cheese and sugar with electric mixer on medium speed until well blended. Gently stir in whipped topping.

**SPOON** into crust. Refrigerate 3 hours or overnight. Top with fresh fruit or cherry pie filling, if desired. Makes 8 servings.

*NOTE: To transfer a purchased crust to your own pie plate, use kitchen shears to carefully cut foil pan. Then, peel pan from crust and place in pie plate.

*Theresa Ann Kreinen
Kraft Creative Kitchens—
Rye Brook, New York*

**Quick tip** I often make this no-bake cheesecake ahead of time and freeze it until I need it. I especially find that a frozen cheesecake is a great idea for toting to picnics! At home before the picnic, place the frozen cheesecake in the refrigerator to thaw for about 8 hours.

## QUICK VANILLA RICE PUDDING

*Enjoy creamy rice pudding in just minutes! For a new twist on this classic dessert, substitute dried cherries, blueberries or cranberries for the raisins.*

☀ Prep time: 5 minutes
Cooking time: 10 minutes plus standing

- 3 cups milk, divided
- 1 cup MINUTE Original Rice, uncooked
- ⅓ cup raisins
- 1 package (4-serving size) JELL-O Vanilla Flavor Instant Pudding & Pie Filling

**BOIL** 1 cup of the milk. Stir in rice and raisins; cover. Let stand 5 minutes.

**MEANWHILE,** prepare pudding as directed on package with remaining 2 cups milk.

**ADD** rice mixture to prepared pudding; stir. Cover surface of pudding with plastic wrap; cool 5 minutes. Stir. Serve warm or chilled. Sprinkle with cinnamon and garnish with cookies, if desired. Makes 6 servings.

*Potluck*

*Picnic*

## JELL-O® FROZEN PUDDING AND GELATIN SNACKS

*Kids love preparing these colorful frozen treats—especially on a rainy day that keeps them indoors. They're so easy to make that even the youngest family member can join in the fun.*

☀ Freezing time: 5 hours

Remove foil lid from JELL-O Pudding or Gelatin Snack. Insert pop stick into pudding or gelatin cup for handle. Freeze 5 hours or overnight until firm. To remove pop from cup, place bottom of cup under warm running water for 15 seconds. Press firmly on bottom of cup to release pop. (Do not twist or pull pop stick.) Once thawed, pops do not refreeze or refrigerate well.

splashing
*Nibbles*

Italian Spinach Dip (recipe, page 28)

# & Dips

Here you'll find recipes for cool dips, spicy nachos and snappy snacks—all simple to prepare and suitable for serving on the patio or at a picnic in the park. What better way to welcome guests at your next summer get-together than with a sampling of tasty appetizers and munchies.

## ITALIAN SPINACH DIP

*To quickly thaw frozen spinach, use the defrost function of your microwave oven, or unwrap the spinach and place in a colander under cold running water until it can be separated with your fingers. Before using, squeeze the thawed spinach with your hands to remove as much liquid as possible (photo, pages 26–27).*

Prep time: 10 minutes plus refrigerating

1   cup KRAFT Mayo Real
      Mayonnaise
1   cup BREAKSTONE'S *or* KNUDSEN
      Sour Cream
1   envelope GOOD SEASONS
      Italian Salad Dressing Mix
1   package (10 ounces) frozen
      chopped spinach, thawed,
      well drained
½   cup chopped red pepper
      (optional)

**MIX** mayo, sour cream and salad dressing mix until well blended. Add spinach and red pepper; mix well. Refrigerate.

**SERVE** in hollowed-out red cabbage with assorted fresh vegetables. Makes 3 cups.

NO OVEN SUMMER

*David Kennedy*
*Kraft Creative Kitchens—*
*Glenview, Illinois*

**Quick tip** For a splash of color, I like to serve dips and spreads in edible containers—hollowed-out round bread loaves, bell peppers, zucchini and small red or green cabbages are great to make into "bowls." After filling it with my dip, I set the "bowl" on a serving plate and surround it with an assortment of crackers, chips or bite-sized veggies.

*Splashing*

## CHEEZY BEER DIP

*Keep a jar of CHEEZ WHIZ and a bottle of beer in your cupboard and you'll be ready for unexpected guests. In just minutes, you can serve them this delicious dip.*

Prep time: 5 minutes   Microwave time: 2 minutes

1   jar (16 ounces) CHEEZ WHIZ
    Pasteurized Process Cheese
    Sauce
⅓   cup beer

**MICROWAVE** process cheese sauce as directed on label.

**MIX** process cheese sauce and beer in bowl, stirring until mixture becomes smooth. Garnish with sliced green onion. Serve with pretzels, breadsticks or green onions. Makes 2 cups.

## PHILLY® CREAMY SALSA DIP

*This creamy dip is a great change of pace from the usual salsa and chips. No one will ever guess that its robust flavor comes from blending only two ingredients!*

☀ Prep time: 10 minutes plus refrigerating

1 package (8 ounces)
   PHILADELPHIA Cream Cheese,
   softened
1 cup TACO BELL HOME ORIGINALS
   Salsa, any variety

**MIX** cream cheese and salsa until well blended. Refrigerate. Garnish with zucchini-and-carrot curl. Serve with crackers, tortilla chips or assorted cut-up vegetables. Makes 2 cups.

NOTE: To make baked tortilla chips, cut flour tortillas into desired shapes. Place, in single layer, on baking sheet. Bake at 350°F for 5 to 10 minutes or until dry and crisp. Remove from baking sheet. Cool on wire rack.

*TACO BELL and HOME ORIGINALS are trademarks owned and licensed by Taco Bell Corp.*

## ANTIPASTO

*The word antipasto means "before the pasta" in Italian. Your guests will savor this appetizer platter of zesty marinated meat, cheese and vegetables before you serve the main dish—whether it's pasta or not!*

☀ Prep time: 15 minutes plus marinating

- 1 bottle (8 ounces) SEVEN SEAS VIVA Italian Dressing
- 1 package (3 ounces) OSCAR MAYER Pepperoni Slices
- 1 can (14 ounces) artichoke hearts, drained, quartered
- 1 cup halved cherry tomatoes
- 1 cup pitted ripe olives
- 10 pepperoncini
- 4 ounces KRAFT Low-Moisture Part-Skim Mozzarella Cheese, cut into ¼-inch sticks

**POUR** dressing over pepperoni, artichoke hearts, tomatoes, olives and pepperoncini; cover. Refrigerate overnight to marinate. Drain, reserving dressing.

**TOSS** pepperoni, vegetables and cheese with reserved dressing. Spoon onto serving platter. Makes 8 to 10 servings.

**Arranged Antipasto:** Marinate and drain pepperoni and vegetables as directed. Arrange pepperoni, vegetables and cheese on platter. Serve with reserved dressing.

**Tossed Antipasto Salad:** Marinate pepperoni and vegetables as directed. Toss pepperoni, vegetables, cheese and 1 package (10 ounces) salad greens. Makes 4 servings.

## FRUIT & CHEESE BITES

*These delicious snacks taste great with a variety of different special fruits such as melons, apples or pears.*

☀ Prep time: 10 minutes

20 table wafer crackers *or any cracker*
1 package (10 ounces) CRACKER BARREL Extra Sharp Natural Cheddar Cheese, thinly sliced
Strawberry halves *or* slices
Kiwi slices, cut in half
¼ cup orange marmalade

**TOP** each cracker with cheese slice, fruit and marmalade. Garnish with fresh mint leaves or sprigs of fresh dill. Makes 20.

## REFRESHING CUCUMBER, DILL 'N CHEDDAR SNACKS

*To add a decorative touch to these snacks, score the cucumber by running the tines of a fork down the length of the cucumber, piercing all the way through the skin. Then, cut the cucumber into slices.*

☀ Prep time: 10 minutes

20 crackers
1 package (10 ounces) CRACKER BARREL Extra Sharp Natural Cheddar Cheese, thinly sliced
Cucumber slices, cut in half
Fresh dill

**TOP** each cracker with cheese slice, cucumber and dill. Makes 20.

Fruit & Cheese Bites
and Refreshing Cucumber, Dill 'N Cheddar Snacks

## NACHO PLATTER OLÉ

*Keep on hand the few ingredients needed for this Mexican-style nibbler, and within minutes, drop-in guests will be enjoying your delicious creation.*

Prep time: 10 minutes    Microwave time: 10 minutes

1 can (16 ounces) TACO BELL HOME ORIGINALS Refried Beans
1 package (8 to 11 ounces) tortilla chips
1 can (15 ounces) chili
1 jar (16 ounces) CHEEZ WHIZ Pasteurized Process Cheese Sauce

**SPREAD** beans onto center of large serving platter.

**ARRANGE** chips around beans. Heat chili as directed on label; pour over beans.

**MICROWAVE** process cheese sauce as directed on label; pour over chili and chips. Garnish with shredded lettuce and chopped red pepper. Serve immediately. Makes 6 to 8 servings.

*TACO BELL and HOME ORIGINALS are trademarks owned and licensed by Taco Bell Corp.*

Jody Matthews
*Kraft Creative Kitchens—
Glenview, Illinois*

**Quick tip** When friends drop by for a visit, I like to serve Nacho Platter Olé. For a footed platter, I turn a saucer or small bowl upside down and place the platter of nachos on top. Then, I set the table with bowls of sour cream, salsa, chopped green onions, guacamole and tomatoes so guests can add more toppings to the nachos.

# stunning

Side dishes take center stage in summer when served alongside simple grilled meats. Creamy potato salads, vibrant vegetable and pasta medleys, and creations bursting with juicy fruit provide the ideal counterpart to any summer meal. And because these recipes assemble so quickly and don't require oven cooking, it's a breeze to treat family and friends to several at one time.

*Spicy 20-Minute Potato Salad (recipe, page 43) and Tangy Broccoli Salad (recipe, page 38) with grilled pork chop.*

# Summertime Sides

## Quick tip

Vegetable salads are best
served crisp and cold. To
keep salads and other
cold foods from wilting
at outdoor summer events,
serve them in chilled bowls.
If possible, place the chilled
bowls in larger bowls filled
with crushed ice to keep
the salads cool longer.

# TANGY BROCCOLI SALAD

*Don't throw away those broccoli stems after removing
the flowerets. Instead, peel off the tough outer skin,
slice thinly and add to your favorite stir-fry recipe
(photo, pages 36–37).*

☀ Prep time: 20 minutes plus refrigerating

- 1 cup MIRACLE WHIP *or*
  MIRACLE WHIP LIGHT Dressing
- 2 tablespoons *each* sugar and
  vinegar
- 1 medium bunch broccoli, cut into
  flowerets (about 6 cups)
- 12 slices OSCAR MAYER Bacon,
  crisply cooked, crumbled
- ½ cup chopped red onion

**MIX** dressing, sugar and vinegar in
large bowl.

**ADD** remaining ingredients; mix lightly.
Refrigerate. Makes 8 servings.

Tangy Broccoli Lettuce Salad: **Prepare salad
as directed, adding 4 cups loosely packed torn
lettuce *or* spinach leaves.**

*Spicy Three Bean Salad*

### SPICY THREE BEAN SALAD

*This new version of an old favorite is as easy as 1, 2, 3—rinse and drain the beans, chop the pepper and toss with the SEVEN SEAS VIVA Italian dressing.*

Prep time: 10 minutes plus refrigerating

1   can (16 ounces) kidney beans, rinsed, drained
1   can (16 ounces) Great Northern beans, rinsed, drained
1   can (16 ounces) black beans, rinsed, drained
½   cup diced green pepper
½   cup diced red pepper
1   cup SEVEN SEAS VIVA Italian Dressing

TOSS all ingredients in large bowl. Refrigerate. Serve in hollowed-out bell pepper halves, if desired. Makes 8 servings.

# BRUSCHETTA SALAD

*Bread salad is a classic Italian dish that is perfect to serve during summer when tomatoes are ripe and flavorful. For best results, use crusty, firm-textured bread.*

Prep time: 10 minutes

3 cups tomato chunks
1 cup SEVEN SEAS VIVA Italian Dressing
1 cup slivered red onion
1 cup (4 ounces) KRAFT 100% Shredded Parmesan Cheese
½ pound day-old bread, cut into cubes

**TOSS** all ingredients. Garnish with fresh basil leaves. Serve immediately. Makes 6 servings.

*Mary Beth Harrington
Kraft Creative Kitchens—
Rye Brook, New York*

**Quick tip** Here are a few of my favorite thirst-quenching summer drinks:

• Mix prepared TANG with softened vanilla ice cream for a dreamy orange drink.

• Stir 2 tablespoons KOOL-AID mix into 8 ounces seltzer water for a fun-flavored soda.

• Pour prepared TANG, KOOL-AID or iced tea over scoops of fruit sherbet or sorbet—refreshing!

*Italian Pasta Salad*

## ITALIAN PASTA SALAD

*When making this or other pasta salads, cook the pasta only
until al dente (still slightly firm), so it doesn't become mushy.*

☀ Prep time: 15 minutes plus refrigerating

3 cups (8 ounces) rotini pasta,
    cooked, drained
2 cups broccoli flowerets
1 bottle (8 ounces) KRAFT House
    Italian with Olive Oil Blend
    Dressing
1 cup (4 ounces) KRAFT 100%
    Grated Parmesan Cheese
½ cup *each* chopped red pepper,
    pitted ripe olives and slivered
    red onion

TOSS all ingredients. Refrigerate.
Makes 8 servings.

## SPICY 20-MINUTE POTATO SALAD

*You can prepare this flavorful potato salad in less time than it takes to make a trip to the deli to purchase potato salad. Quartering the potatoes before cooking them drastically reduces the cooking time (photo, pages 36–37).*

Prep time: 5 minutes plus refrigerating   Cooking time: 14 minutes

5   cups quartered small red potatoes
½   cup KRAFT Mayo Real Mayonnaise *or* MIRACLE WHIP Salad Dressing
⅛   to ¼ teaspoon *each* black pepper, cayenne pepper and salt
⅓   cup *each* sliced celery and sliced green onions

ADD potatoes to boiling water; cook 14 minutes or until fork-tender. Drain.

MIX mayo and seasonings in large bowl.

ADD potatoes, celery and onions; mix lightly. Refrigerate. Makes 6 servings.

Garden Potato Salad: Prepare salad as directed, increasing mayo to ¾ cup and adding ½ teaspoon dill weed. Stir in 1 cup small broccoli flowerets and ½ cup shredded carrot.

NOTE: To use your microwave oven to cook the potatoes, place quartered potatoes and ⅓ cup water in 3-quart microwavable casserole; cover. Microwave on HIGH 14 to 16 minutes or until tender, stirring after 8 minutes. Drain.

NO OVEN SUMMER

Quick tip Prepare pasta or potato salads up to two days in advance by combining the KRAFT Mayo or MIRACLE WHIP with the seasonings and refrigerating this mixture separately from the cooked pasta or potatoes. Then, just before serving, stir the two together for a fresh, great-tasting salad.

## FARMER'S MARKET PASTA SALAD

*A perfect partner to grilled meat, poultry or seafood, this colorful,
farm-fresh salad is sure to win you raves at your next backyard cookout.*

☀ Prep time: 15 minutes

2 cups (4 ounces) rotini pasta,
cooked, drained

1 cup *each* broccoli flowerets,
sliced carrots and halved
cherry tomatoes

¼ cup sliced green onions

1 container (16 ounces)
BREAKSTONE'S *or* KNUDSEN
Cottage Cheese

½ cup KRAFT Ranch Dressing
Salt and pepper

**TOSS** rotini and vegetables in
large bowl.

**ADD** remaining ingredients;
toss lightly. Season to taste with
salt and pepper. Makes 6 to
8 servings.

# BLACK BEAN AND MANGO SALSA

*To choose a perfectly ripe mango for this refreshing recipe, look for one that's firm (not hard) and has smooth, yellow skin tinged with red.*

☀ Prep time: 10 minutes plus refrigerating

- 1 envelope GOOD SEASONS Italian Salad Dressing Mix
- 1 can (16 ounces) black beans, rinsed, drained
- 1 package (10 ounces) frozen corn, thawed
- 1 cup chopped ripe mango
- ½ cup chopped red pepper
- ⅓ cup *each* chopped cilantro and chopped red onion
- ¼ cup lime juice

**MIX** all ingredients in large bowl. Refrigerate.

**SERVE** with grilled chicken or tortilla chips. Makes about 5 cups.

Black Bean and Mango Salad: Prepare mango salsa as directed, adding 1½ cups cooked MINUTE Instant Brown Rice.

## Strawberry & Melon Salad

*To give this succulent salad extra color and flavor, use a combination of melons, such as watermelon, cantaloupe and honeydew.*

Prep time: 20 minutes

| | |
|---|---|
| ¼ | cup orange juice |
| 1 | envelope GOOD SEASONS Italian Salad Dressing Mix |
| ½ | cup oil |
| 2 | tablespoons water |
| 1 | package (10 ounces) salad greens |
| 3 | cups melon balls *or* chunks |
| 1 | cup sliced strawberries |
| 3 | tablespoons sunflower seeds |

**POUR** juice into cruet or medium bowl. Add salad dressing mix, oil and water. Shake vigorously or mix until well blended.

**TOSS** greens, melon, strawberries and dressing in large bowl. Sprinkle with sunflower seeds. Makes 12 servings.

*Debbie Levine*
*Kraft Creative Kitchens—*
*Rye Brook, New York*

**Quick tip** I love fresh summer fruits from the farmer's market. One way I can enjoy these fruits all summer and into autumn is to freeze them at their peak of ripeness. Later, these thawed jewels are a refreshing addition to salads and desserts.

summertime

## COTTAGE BERRY CRUNCH

*Serve this refreshing recipe for breakfast or anytime*
*you have a craving for fresh fruit.*

LIGHT 'N LIVELY Cottage Cheese
Lowfat granola
Banana slices
Assorted berries

**SPOON** cottage cheese into serving bowl. Sprinkle with granola. Top with fruit. Garnish with fresh currants.

## VELVEETA® CHEESY RICE & BROCCOLI

*This simple side dish is easy to adapt to serve a crowd of 12. Just double the ingredients except use only 1½ cups water.*

Prep time: 5 minutes
Cooking time: 10 minutes plus standing

- 1 package (10 ounces) frozen chopped broccoli, thawed, drained
- 1 cup water
- 1½ cups MINUTE White Rice, uncooked
- ½ pound (8 ounces) VELVEETA Pasteurized Process Cheese Spread or VELVEETA LIGHT Pasteurized Process Cheese Product, cut up

**BRING** broccoli and water to boil in medium saucepan. Cook 3 minutes.

**STIR** in rice and process cheese spread; cover. Remove from heat. Let stand 5 minutes. Stir until process cheese spread is melted. Makes 6 servings.

# salad bowl

Ranch Taco Chicken Salad (recipe, page 52)

# Meals

When warm weather prompts appetites to seek lighter fare, turn to these enticing salads. Crisp greens, seasonal fruits, chicken, pasta and tuna are transformed into satisfying lunch or supper entrées. You'll turn to such delights as Summertime Tuna Pasta Salad and Fruity Chicken Salad again and again for cool, carefree dining all summer long.

## RANCH TACO CHICKEN SALAD

*For a great finishing touch, sprinkle ½ cup crushed tortilla chips over this flavorful salad (photo, cover and pages 50–51).*

☀ Prep time: 15 minutes   Cooking time: 8 minutes

1   pound boneless skinless chicken breasts, cut into strips
1   cup TACO BELL HOME ORIGINALS Thick 'N Chunky Salsa, divided
1   package (16 ounces) salad greens
1   cup KRAFT Shredded Cheddar Cheese
1   cup KRAFT FREE Ranch Fat Free Dressing *or* KRAFT Ranch Dressing

COOK and stir chicken in ¼ cup of the salsa in large nonstick skillet on medium-high heat 8 minutes or until chicken is cooked through.

TOSS chicken, greens and cheese on serving platter or in large bowl.

TOP with remaining ¾ cup salsa and dressing before serving. Garnish with tortilla chips. Makes 6 (1½ cup) servings.

Spicy Ranch Taco Chicken Salad: Prepare salad as directed, adding 1 tablespoon chili powder to salsa while cooking chicken.

*TACO BELL and HOME ORIGINALS are trademarks owned and licensed by Taco Bell Corp.*

*Quick tip* Turning this chicken salad into wrap sandwiches is simple. Just fill burrito wraps with the tossed ingredients and roll up—it's so easy! For a change of pace, pair the salad mixture with flavored burrito wraps—like herb, tomato and spinach.

# BACON SPINACH SALAD

*The zesty flavor of KRAFT CATALINA Dressing complements this classic salad of spinach, mushrooms, hard-cooked eggs and bacon.*

Prep time: 15 minutes

5  cups torn spinach
1  cup sliced mushrooms
½  cup thinly sliced red onion wedges
4  slices OSCAR MAYER Bacon, crisply cooked, crumbled
2  hard-cooked eggs, chopped
1  cup KRAFT CATALINA Dressing

**TOSS** all ingredients except dressing in large bowl. Serve with dressing. Makes 6 (1 cup) servings.

Chicken and Bacon Spinach Salad: Prepare salad as directed, adding 2 boneless skinless chicken breasts, grilled, cut into strips.

*Chicken and Bacon Spinach Salad*

## CATALINA® BERRY CHICKEN SALAD

*To make this salad in advance, simply refrigerate the cooked chicken and sliced strawberries in separate containers, then toss together as directed just before serving.*

☀ Prep time: 20 minutes   Cooking time: 8 minutes

1   pound boneless skinless chicken breasts, cut into strips
1   cup KRAFT FREE CATALINA Fat Free Dressing *or* KRAFT CATALINA Dressing, divided
1   package (10 ounces) salad greens *or* spinach
1   cup sliced strawberries
¼   cup sliced almonds

COOK and stir chicken in ¼ cup of the dressing in large skillet on medium heat 8 minutes or until chicken is cooked through.

TOSS greens, strawberries, almonds and chicken in large salad bowl with remaining ¾ cup dressing. Makes 6 (1 cup) servings.

# FRUITY CHICKEN SALAD

*Orzo is a small, rice-shaped pasta that is ideal in salads
and soups or as a side dish in place of rice. You can find
it in the pasta section of the supermarket.*

Prep time: 10 minutes plus refrigerating

1   envelope GOOD SEASONS Honey
    French *or* Italian Salad Dressing
    Mix
¼   cup red wine vinegar
3   cups cooked orzo pasta
2   cups chopped cooked chicken
1   cup red and green seedless
    grapes
½   cup thin carrot strips
    Chopped fresh parsley

**PREPARE** dressing in cruet or small
bowl as directed on envelope using
red wine vinegar for the vinegar.

**MIX** orzo, chicken, grapes and
carrot in large bowl. Add ½ cup of
the dressing; toss to mix well. Cover.

**REFRIGERATE** salad and
remaining dressing at least
2 hours. Just before serving,
mix in remaining dressing.
Serve on lettuce-lined plate.
Sprinkle with parsley.
Makes 6 (1 cup) servings.

Fruity Chicken Salad
Sandwiches: Prepare salad
as directed. Spoon into cut pita
halves *or* onto tortillas and roll up.

## RANCH CHICKEN PASTA SALAD

*A great use for leftover grilled chicken, this simple main-dish salad becomes a complete meal when served with crusty bread and a selection of summer fruits.*

☀ Prep time: 25 minutes

1 package (10.4 ounces) KRAFT Classic Ranch with Bacon Pasta Salad
1 cup chopped cooked chicken *or* turkey
1 cup chopped tomatoes
¼ cup sliced green onions

PREPARE Pasta Salad as directed on package.

STIR in remaining ingredients. Refrigerate or serve immediately. Garnish with fresh herbs. Makes 4 (1 cup) servings.

*Salad Bowl*

## SUMMERTIME TUNA PASTA SALAD

*Shave even more time off this easy recipe by purchasing prepared vegetables from your supermarket salad bar.*

Prep time: 25 minutes plus refrigerating

2 cups pasta (such as bowties, mafalda *or* macaroni), cooked, drained

1 can (6 ounces) white tuna in water, drained, flaked

1 cup MIRACLE WHIP *or* MIRACLE WHIP LIGHT Dressing

1 cup *each* broccoli flowerets, chopped carrots and sliced celery *or* chopped seeded cucumber

1 teaspoon dill weed

½ teaspoon pepper

**MIX** all ingredients. Refrigerate several hours or overnight. Serve on lettuce-lined platter. Garnish with halved lemon slices. Makes 6 (1 cup) servings.

Meals

# sun-sational Sandwiches

*Western Bologna Sub (recipe, page 60)*

Sandwiches and summer go hand in hand. Portable and ready to eat in minutes, sandwiches are a great way to get a meal on the table fast without heating up the kitchen.

## WESTERN BOLOGNA SUB

*Turn ordinary bologna into a hearty meal by whipping up this zesty sub sandwich. The smoky flavors of barbecue sauce and bacon will transport you to the Old West (photo, pages 58–59).*

☀ Prep time: 10 minutes

1 small loaf (8 ounces) French *or* sourdough bread, cut in half lengthwise
2 tablespoons KRAFT Mayo Real Mayonnaise
2 tablespoons KRAFT Original Barbecue Sauce
Leaf lettuce
1 package (8 ounces) OSCAR MAYER Bologna
Thinly sliced onion
4 slices OSCAR MAYER Bacon, crisply cooked

SPREAD bottom half of bread loaf with mayo. Spread top half of bread loaf with barbecue sauce.

LAYER bottom with lettuce, bologna, onion, bacon and additional lettuce. Cover with top half of bread. Cut into 4 pieces. Secure with garnished toothpick, if desired. Makes 4 servings.

*Mary J. Brooks*
*Kraft Creative Kitchens—*
*Rye Brook, New York*

## Quick tip
Instead of purchasing decorative picks, I make my own to add a special touch to sandwiches and appetizers. To make them, I use small cookie cutters or, for simple shapes, a small paring knife to cut shapes from strips of red, orange, yellow or green pepper or citrus peel. Then, I just slide the shapes onto wooden or plastic picks.

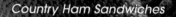
*Country Ham Sandwiches*

## COUNTRY HAM SANDWICHES

*Lunch is easy when you start with a hearty sandwich and add
a side-dish salad, such as Great American Potato Salad (recipe, page 8)
or Spicy Three Bean Salad (recipe, page 39).*

Prep time: 10 minutes

½ cup MIRACLE WHIP Salad
    Dressing *or* KRAFT Mayo Real
    Mayonnaise
½ teaspoon garlic powder
½ teaspoon pepper
8 slices whole wheat bread
    Lettuce and tomato slices
    (optional)
1 package (6 ounces)
    OSCAR MAYER Smoked
    Cooked Ham
8 KRAFT Singles Process Cheese
    Food

**MIX** salad dressing and
seasonings in small bowl.

**SPREAD** on bread slices.

**LAYER** 4 of the bread slices
each with lettuce, tomato, ham
and 2 process cheese food slices.
Top with second bread slices.
Makes 4 sandwiches.

Country Ham Apple Sandwiches:
Prepare sandwiches as directed,
omitting garlic powder and pepper
and substituting apple slices for
tomato slices.

*Sun-sational Sandwiches* **61**

*Easy Turkey Wrap Sandwich and Grilled Turkey Club*

## EASY TURKEY WRAP SANDWICH

*Tote these make-ahead tortilla roll-ups anywhere your summer travels may take you—to the zoo, the beach or a picnic in your own backyard.*

KRAFT Mayo Real Mayonnaise
Flour tortilla
Leaf lettuce
LOUIS RICH CARVING BOARD
   Oven Roasted Turkey Breast
KRAFT Singles Process Cheese
   Food
Tomato slices

**SPREAD** mayo on tortilla.

**TOP** with lettuce, turkey, process cheese food and tomato. Fold up sides of tortilla to center, slightly overlapping. Secure with toothpick, if desired.

## GRILLED TURKEY CLUB

*Toasting this turkey, bacon and cheese sandwich in a skillet is a great way to prepare a hot meal without turning on the oven.*

☀ Prep time: 5 minutes  Cooking time: 10 minutes

2  slices bread
4  slices LOUIS RICH
     CARVING BOARD Thin Carved
     Oven Roasted Turkey Breast
1  tomato slice
2  slices OSCAR MAYER Bacon,
     crisply cooked
2  KRAFT Singles Process Cheese
     Food
     Butter *or* margarine, softened

**TOP** 1 bread slice with turkey, tomato, bacon, process cheese food and second bread slice.

**SPREAD** outside of sandwich with butter.

**COOK** in skillet on medium heat until lightly browned on both sides. Cut into triangles. Secure with garnished toothpicks, if desired. Makes 1 sandwich.

*Sara Vanderleest
Kraft Creative Kitchens—
Glenview, Illinois*

# Quick tip It's easy

to add flair to summer drinks.

For pretty ice cubes, I drop

berries or small pieces of fruit

into the compartments of an

ice cube tray, fill the tray with

water and freeze. To make

fun stirrers, I put vegetable or

fruit chunks on small skewers.

## GRILLED HAM & CHEESE

*The addition of smoked ham transforms
the ever-popular grilled cheese sandwich
from a lunch treat into a light supper.*

Prep time: 5 minutes   Cooking time: 10 minutes

- 2  slices bread
- 2  KRAFT Singles Process Cheese
     Food
- 3  slices OSCAR MAYER Smoked
     Cooked Ham
     MIRACLE WHIP Salad Dressing
     *or* KRAFT Mayo Real Mayonnaise

**TOP** 1 bread slice with 1 process cheese
food slice, ham, second process cheese
food slice and second bread slice.

**SPREAD** outside of sandwich with salad
dressing or mayonnaise.

**COOK** in skillet on medium heat until
lightly browned on both sides. Makes
1 sandwich.

Dressed-Up Grilled Ham & Cheese:
Prepare sandwich as directed, spreading Dijon
mustard between bread slices and adding
tomato slices before cooking.

# GARDEN TUNA MELTS

*If your supermarket or local farmer's market features fresh basil and oregano, mince about 1½ teaspoons of each and substitute the fresh for the dried herbs in this sensational grilled tuna-cheese sandwich.*

Prep time: 10 minutes   Cooking time: 10 minutes

1   can (6 ounces) white tuna in water, drained, flaked
⅓   cup KRAFT Mayo Real Mayonnaise *or* MIRACLE WHIP Salad Dressing
¼   cup *each* chopped onion and green pepper
½   teaspoon *each* dried basil leaves and dried oregano leaves
8   slices bread
4   KRAFT Singles Process Cheese Food

**MIX** tuna, mayo, onion, green pepper and seasonings.

**TOP** 4 bread slices each with 1 process cheese food slice, tuna mixture and second bread slice. Spread outsides of sandwiches with additional mayo or softened butter.

**COOK** in skillet on medium heat until lightly browned on both sides. Makes 4 sandwiches.

Carrot and Cucumber Tuna Melts: Prepare sandwiches as directed, substituting chopped carrot and cucumber for onion and green pepper.

*Quick tip* When a family day at the beach is put off by rain clouds, create your own indoor beach party. Rent a beach-themed movie, lay down blankets or beach towels and enjoy your picnic lunch indoors—and ant free!

Cool & Satisfying

TACO BELL® HOME ORIGINALS® 2-Step Tacos
(recipe, page 70)

# Main Dishes

When the temperature outside is rising, look no further for fast and easy meal ideas. These no oven main dishes are flavorful flashes in the pan—sure to please hungry appetites while keeping you cool as a cucumber.

*April Myslinski*
*Kraft Creative Kitchens—*
*Glenview, Illinois*

**Quick tip** Here's the neat way I serve taco top-

pings at my house. I place the cheese, salsa and lettuce in

the separate cups of a muffin tin. This way there's only one

item to pass around the table. A muffin tin also works great

for holding condiments for hamburgers and hot dogs.

## TACO BELL® HOME ORIGINALS® 2-STEP TACOS

*In addition to cheese, salsa and lettuce, try topping your taco with sour cream, ripe olives and purchased guacamole (photo, pages 68–69).*

You only need:
- 1 pound ground beef
- 1 package (1.25 ounces) TACO BELL HOME ORIGINALS Taco Seasoning Mix
- 1 package (4.5 ounces) TACO BELL HOME ORIGINALS Taco Shells
  KRAFT Shredded Cheese
  TACO BELL HOME ORIGINALS Thick 'N Chunky Salsa
  Packaged cut-up lettuce

**1. PREP IT QUICK!** Cook meat; drain. Add seasoning mix; prepare as directed on package.

**2. PILE ON THE FUN!™** Place bowls of cooked meat and remaining ingredients on your table. Pass the heated taco shells and let everyone build their own! Makes 6 servings.

NOTE: You can substitute 1 package (10.75 ounces) TACO BELL HOME ORIGINALS Taco Dinner Kit for the seasoning mix, taco shells and salsa. It's all in the kit!

*TACO BELL and HOME ORIGINALS are trademarks owned and licensed by Taco Bell Corp.*

*Chicken 'N Peppers Pasta Skillet*

## CHICKEN 'N PEPPERS PASTA SKILLET

*Minimize last-minute preparation by cooking the pasta ahead, rinsing it in cold water and refrigerating it until ready to prepare this flavorful recipe.*

Prep time: 10 minutes   Cooking time: 10 minutes plus standing

1   pound boneless skinless chicken breasts, chopped
1   green pepper, cut into thin strips
1   jar (14 ounces) spaghetti sauce (about 1½ cups)
2   cups (4 ounces) rotini pasta, cooked, drained
2   cups KRAFT Classic Garlic Italian Style Shredded Cheese, divided

SPRAY large skillet with no stick cooking spray. Add chicken; cook and stir 5 minutes. Add green pepper; cook and stir until chicken is cooked through and green pepper is tender.

STIR in sauce, rotini and 1 cup of the cheese. Sprinkle with remaining 1 cup cheese; cover. Let stand 1 to 2 minutes or until cheese is melted. Makes 6 servings.

## VELVEETA®
## SALSA MAC 'N CHEESE

*Salsa adds a punch of Tex-Mex flavor
to this creamy mac 'n cheese.*

☀ Prep time: 10 minutes   Cooking time: 15 minutes

- 1   pound ground beef
- 1   jar (16 ounces) TACO BELL
     HOME ORIGINALS Thick 'N Chunky Salsa
- 1¾  cups water
- 1   package (7 ounces) elbow macaroni,
     uncooked
- ¾  pound (12 ounces) VELVEETA
     Pasteurized Process Cheese Spread,
     cut up

BROWN meat in large skillet; drain.

ADD salsa and water. Bring to boil.
Stir in macaroni. Reduce heat to
medium-low; cover with tight-fitting lid.
Simmer 8 to 10 minutes or until macaroni
is tender.

ADD process cheese spread; stir until
melted. Makes 6 servings.

*TACO BELL and HOME ORIGINALS are
trademarks owned and licensed by
Taco Bell Corp.*

## Quick tip

To keep kids entertained

while you are preparing

dinner, set out large

sheets of white paper

and crayons and

ask them to make

lace mats for everyone.

By the time dinner is

ready, the table will be

covered with colorful,

original works of art.

Ann Conway-Purcell
Kraft Creative Kitchens—
Glenview, Illinois

**Quick tip** To easily marinate
chicken and steaks, I freeze the
poultry or meat right in a marinade.
First, I wash the pieces and pat dry.
Then, I place them in a large reseal-
able plastic freezer bag with enough
SEVEN SEAS VIVA Italian Dressing to
coat and place the bags in the
freezer. To serve, I thaw the pieces
overnight in the refrigerator before
cooking. The poultry or meat
marinates as it thaws.

## 15 Minute Chicken & Rice Dinner

*It's true—you can have dinner on the table
in just 15 minutes with this super-simple
one-dish meal.*

Prep/Cooking time: 15 minutes

1    tablespoon oil*
4    boneless skinless chicken breast
     halves (about 1¼ pounds)
1    can (10¾ ounces) condensed
     cream of chicken soup
1    soup can (1⅓ cups) water *or* milk
2    cups MINUTE Original Rice,
     uncooked

**HEAT** oil in large nonstick skillet on
medium-high heat. Add chicken;
cover. Cook 4 minutes on each
side or until cooked through.

**REMOVE** chicken from skillet. Stir
in soup and water. Bring to boil.

**STIR** in rice. Top with chicken;
cover. Cook on low heat
5 minutes. Garnish with fresh
oregano. Makes 4 servings.

*NOTE: Increase oil to 2 tablespoons
if using regular skillet.

## TEX-MEX FAJITAS

*To use a microwave to warm the tortillas for these family-pleasing fajitas, wrap them loosely in waxed paper, then microwave on HIGH for 30 to 40 seconds.*

Prep time: 20 minutes   Cooking time: 10 minutes

½   pound boneless skinless chicken breasts, cut into thin strips
1   clove garlic, minced
1   medium green *or* red pepper, cut into strips
½   cup sliced red onion
1   cup KRAFT Finely Shredded Colby & Monterey Jack Cheese
6   flour tortillas (6 inch), warmed TACO BELL HOME ORIGINALS Thick 'N Chunky Salsa

SPRAY skillet with no stick cooking spray. Add chicken and garlic; cook and stir on medium-high heat 5 minutes.

ADD green pepper and onion; cook 4 to 5 minutes or until chicken is cooked through and vegetables are tender-crisp.

PLACE ¼ cup chicken mixture and ¼ cup cheese on center of each tortilla; fold in half. Serve with salsa. Makes 6 servings.

*TACO BELL and HOME ORIGINALS are trademarks owned and licensed by Taco Bell Corp.*

**76** *Cool & Satisfying Main Dishes*

## ALL AMERICAN DELUXE CHEESEBURGERS

*Before shaping the burgers, dampen your hands—this helps prevent the meat from sticking to them.*

☀ Prep time: 10 minutes   Grilling time: 12 minutes

- 1 pound ground beef
- 8 KRAFT Deluxe Process American Cheese Slices
- 2 tablespoons KRAFT Thousand Island Dressing
- 2 tablespoons KRAFT Mayo Real Mayonnaise
- 4 Kaiser *or* hamburger rolls, split, toasted
  Lettuce
  Tomato and red onion slices
  CLAUSSEN Classic Dill Super Slices for Burgers

**SHAPE** meat into 4 patties. Place patties on grill over hot coals. Grill 8 to 12 minutes or to desired doneness, turning occasionally.

**TOP** each patty with 2 process cheese slices; cover. Continue grilling until process cheese is melted.

**MIX** dressing and mayo in small bowl. Spread 1 tablespoon dressing mixture on each roll. Fill rolls with cheeseburgers, lettuce, tomato, onion and pickles. Makes 4 sandwiches.

**Top of Stove Method:** Shape meat as directed. Cook patties in skillet on medium heat 8 to 12 minutes, turning occasionally or to desired doneness. Continue as directed.

# CHEESEBURGER RICE

*All the fixings for a cheeseburger are combined with rice to create
a savory skillet dish that's sure to become a family favorite.*

Prep time: 10 minutes   Cooking time: 15 minutes

| | |
|---|---|
| 1 pound lean ground beef | **BROWN** meat in large skillet on medium-high heat; drain. |
| 1¾ cups water | |
| ⅔ cup catsup | |
| 1 tablespoon KRAFT Pure Prepared Mustard | **ADD** water, catsup and mustard. Bring to boil. |
| 2 cups MINUTE Original Rice, uncooked | |
| 1 cup KRAFT Shredded Cheddar Cheese | **STIR** in rice. Sprinkle with cheese; cover. Cook on low heat 5 minutes. Makes 4 servings. |

## CHEESY CHICKEN & BROCCOLI MACARONI

*The whole family will love this chicken and broccoli version of macaroni and cheese—it's a great way to get the kids to eat their meat and veggies!*

☀ Prep time: 10 minutes   Cooking time: 15 minutes

4 boneless skinless chicken breast halves (about 1¼ pounds), cut into chunks
1 can (13¾ ounces) chicken broth
1 package (7 ounces) elbow macaroni, uncooked
¾ pound (12 ounces) VELVEETA Pasteurized Process Cheese Spread, cut up
1 package (10 ounces) frozen chopped broccoli, thawed

SPRAY large skillet with no stick cooking spray. Add chicken; cook and stir 2 minutes or until chicken is no longer pink.

STIR in broth. Bring to boil. Stir in macaroni. Reduce heat to medium-low; cover. Simmer 8 to 10 minutes or until macaroni is tender.

ADD process cheese spread and broccoli; stir until process cheese spread is melted. Makes 6 servings.

# sizzling grill Favorites

Grilled Chicken Caesar Salad (recipe, page 84)
and Grilled Bread (recipe, page 91)

Everything seems to taste better when cooked outdoors on the grill. But if you've been grilling the same foods summer after summer, it's time to add spark to your repertoire. Try Meat and Potatoes Salad, Grilled Bread, Grilled Italian Chicken Breasts and the other tantalizing recipes in this chapter to put sizzle back into your summer meals.

# Grilling Tips

Grilling is one of the easiest and most pleasant ways to cook in the summer. To ensure great results, follow these hints:

● Always make sure the grill rack is clean before grilling. To prevent foods from sticking to the grill rack during cooking, spray the unheated rack *away from the fire* with no stick cooking spray or brush with oil.

● Use tongs or a spatula, rather than a fork, to move and turn the meat. Piercing the meat with a fork causes the juices to escape, which makes the meat less flavorful and less moist.

● To add extra flavor to grilled foods, soak aromatic hardwood chips (hickory, mesquite or apple) or bunches of fresh herbs (rosemary, oregano or tarragon) in water and add to the coals right before cooking.

● To ensure food safety, always remove cooked food from the grill onto a clean plate. Never place the cooked food on a plate that had raw food on it.

● To easily clean the rack after using, place a sheet of aluminum foil, shiny-side down, on the rack over the glowing coals. Leave the foil on for 5 minutes. When you remove the foil, any food particles still on the grill rack will brush right off.

## Testing Charcoal Temperature

*Different foods require different temperatures to cook properly. An easy way to judge coal temperature is to carefully hold your hand, palm-side down, about 4 inches above the coals or drip pan. Count the number of seconds (one thousand one, one thousand two, etc.) you can hold your hand in that position before the heat forces you to pull it away (see chart at right).*

| Seconds | Coal Temperature |
|---------|------------------|
| 2 | Hot |
| 3 | Medium-Hot |
| 4 | Medium |
| 5 | Medium-Low |
| 6 | Low |

# GRILLED ITALIAN CHICKEN BREASTS

*To save time and dishes when making these crumb-coated chicken breasts, combine the crumb mixture in a large plastic bag. After dipping each piece of chicken in butter, add it to the bag and gently shake to coat. Discard crumbs remaining in bag.*

☀ Prep time: 10 minutes   Grilling time: 20 minutes

½ cup (2 ounces) PARM PLUS! Seasoning Blend*

¼ cup dry bread crumbs

6 boneless skinless chicken breast halves (about 2 pounds)

2 tablespoons butter *or* margarine, melted

**MIX** seasoning blend and bread crumbs.

**DIP** chicken in butter; coat with seasoning blend mixture. Place on greased grill over medium-hot coals.

**GRILL** 20 minutes or until cooked through, turning occasionally. Makes 6 servings.

*NOTE: To substitute KRAFT 100% Grated Parmesan Cheese for PARM PLUS! Seasoning Blend, use ½ cup (2 ounces) KRAFT 100% Grated Parmesan Cheese and 1 teaspoon *each* dried oregano leaves and parsley flakes and ¼ teaspoon *each* paprika, salt and pepper to bread crumb mixture.

## GRILLED CHICKEN CAESAR SALAD

*The first Caesar salad is credited to Caesar Cardini, an Italian chef whose restaurant was in Tijuana, Mexico. Here, the addition of grilled chicken turns this world-famous salad into a hearty entrée (photo, pages 80–81).*

☀ Prep time: 15 minutes

8 cups torn romaine lettuce *or* 1 package (10 ounces) mixed *or* romaine salad greens
1 pound boneless skinless chicken breasts, grilled, cut into strips
1 cup seasoned croutons
½ cup (2 ounces) KRAFT 100% Shredded *or* Grated Parmesan Cheese
¾ cup KRAFT Classic Caesar Dressing *or* KRAFT Caesar Italian Dressing*

**TOSS** lettuce, chicken, croutons and cheese in large salad bowl with dressing.

**SERVE** with fresh lemon wedges and fresh ground pepper, if desired. Garnish with curled lemon peel and tomato wedges. Makes 6 (1½ cup) servings.

*NOTE: KRAFT FREE Classic Caesar Fat Free Dressing *or* KRAFT FREE Caesar Italian Fat Free Dressing can be substituted for regular dressing.

Grilled Chicken Caesar Salad with Garlic: Prepare salad as directed, except cut garlic clove in half; rub cut edges on inside of serving bowl before adding greens.

Grilled Chicken Mediterranean-Style Salad: Prepare salad as directed. Toss salad with pitted ripe olives *or* plum tomato wedges.

Sizzling Grill

*Mary Lee-Brody*
*Kraft Creative Kitchens—*
*Rye Brook, New York*

$\mathcal{Q}$uick tip I've found I can cut down on my trips to the supermarket by relying on my refrigerator and freezer to store raw and cooled meats and poultry. The chart below shows how long food will keep refrigerated and frozen.

| Food | Refrigerator | Freezer |
|------|-------------|---------|
| Soups/Stews | 3 to 4 days | 2 to 3 months |
| Raw ground beef | 1 to 2 days | 3 to 4 months |
| Raw pork chops | 3 to 5 days | 4 to 6 months |
| Raw lamb roasts | 3 to 5 days | 6 to 9 months |
| Cooked leftover meat | 3 to 4 days | 2 to 3 months |
| Fresh, whole raw poultry | 1 to 2 days | 1 year |
| Cooked poultry dishes | 3 to 4 days | 4 to 6 months |

## MEAT AND POTATOES SALAD

*This robust salad is actually a main dish, side dish and salad all in one! Marinated steak and potatoes are grilled, then tossed with salad greens and Italian dressing for an enticing summer meal (photo, pages 2–3).*

Prep time: 10 minutes plus marinating   Grilling time: 15 minutes

1½ cups SEVEN SEAS VIVA Italian Dressing, divided
1 pound beef sirloin steak
½ pound new potatoes, cut into quarters
1 package (10 ounces) salad greens
1 cup tomato wedges
½ cup thinly sliced red onion

**POUR** 1 cup of the dressing over steak; cover. Refrigerate 4 hours or overnight to marinate. Drain; discard dressing.

**PLACE** potatoes in double layer of heavy-duty aluminum foil to form pouch; top with remaining ½ cup dressing. Place steak and potato pouch on greased grill over medium coals.

**GRILL** 15 minutes or until steak is cooked to desired doneness, turning occasionally. Cut steak across grain into thin strips. Toss greens, tomato, onion, steak strips and potatoes. Makes 4 servings.

## MEAT LOVER'S BARBECUED STEAK

*Turn this tasty dish into a hearty sandwich by slicing the steak and then piling it and the onions into a French roll.*

☀ Prep time: 5 minutes   Grilling time: 20 minutes

1½  pounds beef steak, 1 inch thick
1   clove garlic, halved
1   large onion, cut into ¼-inch slices
1   cup KRAFT Original Barbecue Sauce *or* KRAFT THICK 'N SPICY Original Barbecue Sauce

**RUB** both sides of steak with garlic clove halves.

**PLACE** steak and onion slices on greased grill over hot coals.

**GRILL,** uncovered, 15 to 20 minutes or to desired doneness, brushing steak and onion slices frequently with barbecue sauce and turning occasionally. Makes 4 to 6 servings.

Broiler Method: Prepare steak as directed, except place steak and onion slices on greased rack of broiler pan. Broil 15 to 20 minutes or to desired doneness, brushing steak and onion slices frequently with barbecue sauce and turning occasionally.

*Quick tip* Having a big party? Use a kiddie swimming pool filled with ice as a large cooler. Set it alongside the buffet table to keep pitchers and cans of beverages well chilled. Or, if you have a large buffet table, put the ice-filled pool on your table and nestle bowls of salads in the ice.

*Sizzling*

## BBQ CHICKEN WRAP SANDWICHES

*To make slicing an onion easier and safer, first remove a small slice from one side of the onion. This creates a flat base so the onion won't roll around as you slice it.*

Prep time: 15 minutes   Grilling time: 12 minutes

1 pound boneless skinless chicken breasts
2 medium green peppers, quartered
1 medium onion, sliced
1 cup KRAFT Original Barbecue Sauce
8 flour tortillas (6 inch) *or* 4 flour tortillas (10 inch), warmed

**PLACE** chicken and vegetables on greased grill over medium-hot coals.

**GRILL** chicken 10 to 12 minutes or until cooked through and vegetables 8 to 10 minutes, brushing each frequently with sauce and turning occasionally.

**SLICE** chicken and vegetables into thin strips. Divide filling among tortillas. Fold up sides of tortilla to center, slightly overlapping. Secure with toothpick, if desired. Serve with additional sauce, if desired. Makes 4 servings.

BBQ Pork Wrap Sandwiches: Prepare sandwiches as directed, substituting boneless pork chops for chicken. Grill 16 minutes or until cooked through, turning occasionally.

*Robin Ross*
*Kraft Creative Kitchens—*
*Glenview, Illinois*

**Quick tip** When I've purchased a basketful of vegetables at the farmer's market, I grill them brushed with KRAFT Italian dressing! Just like the peppers and onions in the recipe above, eggplant, zucchini, yellow squash, asparagus and mushrooms are also delicious hot off the grill.

*Cheezy Dogs*

## CHEEZY DOGS

*Delicious drizzles of CHEEZ WHIZ dress up an
all-time summer favorite—grilled hot dogs.*

Prep time: 5 minutes   Grilling time: 6 minutes

1 package (16 ounces)
   OSCAR MAYER Bun-Length Beef
   Franks *or* Wieners
8 hot dog buns
1 cup CHEEZ WHIZ Pasteurized
   Process Cheese Sauce,
   microwaved as directed on
   label

**GRILL** franks 6 minutes or until
heated through.

**PLACE** franks in buns. Drizzle
about 2 tablespoons process
cheese sauce over each frank.
Makes 8 sandwiches.

*Grill*

## GRILLED BREAD

*Bread on the grill? You bet! Once you take a bite you'll be hooked. Put the bread slices in a grill basket and you can turn them all at once (photo, pages 80–81).*

☀ Prep time: 5 minutes   Grilling time: 6 minutes

1 bottle (8 ounces) KRAFT House Italian with Olive Oil Blend Dressing
1 loaf French bread, cut into slices

**SPREAD** dressing generously over cut surfaces of bread. Place on grill over medium coals.

**GRILL** 3 minutes on each side or until toasted. Serve with salads or grilled meats. Makes 12 servings.

**Bruschetta in a breeze!** Prepare as directed. Top grilled bread with chopped tomato and sliced green onions.

**Italian bread in an instant!** Cut bread in half lengthwise. Prepare as directed, placing bread, dressing-side down, on grill. Grill until toasted; top with sliced plum tomatoes, fresh basil and KRAFT Shredded Mozzarella Cheese. Place on grill, topped-side up; cover. Grill an additional 5 minutes.

**A super sandwich!** Cut bread in half lengthwise. Prepare as directed, placing bread, dressing-side down, on grill. Grill until toasted; top bread with OSCAR MAYER Sliced Meats, KRAFT Singles Process Cheese Food, lettuce and tomatoes.

*Quick tip* Grilled Parmesan Corn makes a great side dish with grilled foods. Soak unhusked corn in water for 2 hours, then grill it for 20 minutes or until tender. Turn corn frequently to prevent burning. Brush the corn with softened butter, then roll it in KRAFT 100% Grated Parmesan Cheese. Your family will love it!

# Favorites

# INDEX

# Metric Chart

## Metric Cooking Hints

By making a few conversions, cooks in Australia, Canada, and the United Kingdom can use the recipes in *No Oven Summer™ Sensations* with confidence. The charts on this page provide a guide for converting measurements from the U.S. customary system, which is used throughout this book, to the imperial and metric systems. There also is a conversion table for oven temperatures to accommodate the differences in oven calibrations.

**Product Differences:** Most of the ingredients called for in the recipes in this book are available in English-speaking countries. However, some are known by different names. Here are some common American ingredients and their possible counterparts:

- Sugar is granulated or castor sugar.
- Powdered sugar is icing sugar.
- All-purpose flour is plain household flour or white flour. When self-rising flour is used in place of all-purpose flour in a recipe that calls for leavening, omit the leavening agent (baking soda or baking powder) and salt.
- Light-colored corn syrup is golden syrup.
- Cornstarch is cornflour.
- Baking soda is bicarbonate of soda.
- Vanilla is vanilla essence.
- Green, red or yellow sweet peppers are capsicums.
- Golden raisins are sultanas.

**Volume and Weight:** Americans traditionally use cup measures for liquid and solid ingredients. The chart, above right, shows the approximate imperial and metric equivalents. If you are accustomed to weighing solid ingredients, the following approximate equivalents will be helpful.

- 1 cup butter, castor sugar, or rice = 8 ounces = about 250 grams
- 1 cup flour = 4 ounces = about 125 grams
- 1 cup icing sugar = 5 ounces = about 150 grams
Spoon measures are used for smaller amounts of ingredients. Although the size of the tablespoon varies slightly in different countries, for practical purposes and for recipes in this book, a straight substitution is all that's necessary.

Measurements made using cups or spoons always should be level unless stated otherwise.

## EQUIVALENTS: U.S. = AUSTRALIA/U.K.

| | |
|---|---|
| ⅛ teaspoon = 0.5 ml | ⅔ cup = ½ cup = 5 fluid ounces = 150 ml |
| ¼ teaspoon = 1 ml | ¾ cup = ⅔ cup = 6 fluid ounces = 180 ml |
| ½ teaspoon = 2 ml | 1 cup = ¾ cup = 8 fluid ounces = 240 ml |
| 1 teaspoon = 5 ml | 1¼ cups = 1 cup |
| 1 tablespoon = 1 tablespoon | 2 cups = 1 pint |
| ¼ cup = 2 tablespoons = 2 fluid ounces = 60 ml | 1 quart = 1 litre |
| ⅓ cup = ¼ cup = 3 fluid ounces = 90 ml | ½ inch = 1.27 cm |
| ½ cup = ⅓ cup = 4 fluid ounces = 120 ml | 1 inch = 2.54 cm |

## BAKING PAN SIZES

| American | Metric |
|---|---|
| 8x1½-inch round baking pan | 20x4-centimetre cake tin |
| 9x1½-inch round baking pan | 23x3.5-centimetre cake tin |
| 11x7x1½-inch baking pan | 28x18x4-centimetre baking tin |
| 13x9x2-inch baking pan | 30x20x3-centimetre baking tin |
| 2-quart rectangular baking dish | 30x20x3-centimetre baking tin |
| 15x10x1-inch baking pan | 30x25x2-centimetre baking tin (Swiss roll tin) |
| 9-inch pie plate | 22x4- or 23x4-centimetre pie plate |
| 7- or 8-inch springform pan | 18- or 20-centimetre springform or loose-bottom cake tin |
| 9x5x3-inch loaf pan | 23x13x7-centimetre or 2-pound narrow loaf tin or paté tin |
| 1½-quart casserole | 1.5-litre casserole |
| 2-quart casserole | 2-litre casserole |

## OVEN TEMPERATURE EQUIVALENTS

| Fahrenheit Setting | Celsius Setting* | Gas Setting |
|---|---|---|
| 300°F | 150°C | Gas Mark 2 (slow) |
| 325°F | 160°C | Gas Mark 3 (moderately slow) |
| 350°F | 180°C | Gas Mark 4 (moderate) |
| 375°F | 190°C | Gas Mark 5 (moderately hot) |
| 400°F | 200°C | Gas Mark 6 (hot) |
| 425°F | 220°C | Gas Mark 7 |
| 450°F | 230°C | Gas Mark 8 (very hot) |
| Broil | | Grill |

* Electric and gas ovens may be calibrated using Celsius. However, for an electric oven, increase the Celsius setting 10 to 20 degrees when cooking above 160°C. For convection or forced-air ovens (gas or electric), lower the temperature setting 10°C when cooking at all heat levels.

Choose from the family of KRAFT products to make the deliciously easy recipes in this cookbook. You'll find recipes using BREAKSTONE'S Sour Cream and Cottage Cheese, CHEEZ WHIZ Cheese Sauce, CLAUSSEN Pickles, COOL WHIP Whipped Topping, CRACKER BARREL Cheeses, GOOD SEASONS Salad Dressing Mixes, JELL-O Desserts, KNUDSEN Dairy Products, KRAFT Barbecue Sauces, KRAFT Cheeses, KRAFT Mayo and Dressings, KRAFT Pasta Salads, KRAFT Mustard, LIGHT 'N LIVELY Cottage Cheese, LOUIS RICH Turkey Breast Products, MINUTE Rice, MIRACLE WHIP Salad Dressings, OSCAR MAYER Meats, PHILADELPHIA Cream Cheese, SEVEN SEAS Salad Dressings, TACO BELL HOME ORIGINALS Products and VELVEETA Cheese Spread.

**Editorial and Design**
Meredith Custom Publishing

**Recipe Development and Testing**
Kraft Creative Kitchens

**Food Styling**
Amy Andrews, Kathy Aragaki,
Carol Parik, Bonnie Rabert

**Photography**
Tom Firak, Jose Pascual, Joe Polivka

**Prop Styling**
Bonnie Kaplan, Cindy Neberz

Produced by Meredith Custom
Publishing, 1716 Locust Street,
Des Moines, IA 50309-3023

TACO BELL and HOME ORIGINALS are
trademarks owned and licensed by
Taco Bell Corp.